THE EFFECT OF DIVORCE ON CHILDREN UNDER THE AGE OF 18

Pastor Lorenzo Barr

Pastor of Resurrection Faith Baptist Church Dallas, Texas

ISBN 979-8-88644-494-0 (Paperback)
ISBN 979-8-88644-496-4 (Hardcover)
ISBN 979-8-88644-495-7 (Digital)

Covenant Books
11661 Hwy 707
Murrells Inlet, SC 29576
www.covenantbooks.com

ABSTRACT

The turn of the century has transformed all the social and political institutions significantly; however, the institution that has been affected the most is the institution of family and marriage. The changing norms and cultures, the changing concepts regarding parenting, and the spiking graphs of divorce highlighted the alarming situation of the declining institution of marriage.

The problem has been further invigorated by the declined institution of religion. The following research will extensively develop on the issue of the collapsing institution of marriage and the increased divorce ration in the society. These facts will then be connected with the way these practices of divorce affect children psychologically with special focus on those under eighteen years.

The research will be divided into chapters that will proceed step-by-step toward the conclusions. The research shall also include the interview data of the individuals including the parents and children to determine how they have perceived and accepted this change that occurs with finalization of marriage. Graphs and statistical evidences will be used.

CONTENTS

INTRODUCTION

Marriage as an institution is crucial to human existence. It is a significant avenue for man to partake in creative activities of God via procreation. The command "be fruitful and multiply" (Genesis 1:28) can only be fulfilled in the context of marriage. Besides, marriage is a precursor to family formation.

Given this, every culture recognizes its importance in spite of relativism. Christian marriages are expected to be a life contract hence the phrase "till death do us part." In other words, on no account may divorce or separation be the option no matter the circumstances. However, the rate of divorce and separation among contemporary Christians is worrisome as marriages do crash over irreconcilable differences.

The socioethical effects of divorce are obvious, and solutions are apparently elusive in spite of several measures being taken by the church, marriage counselors, and other concerned individuals or groups to minimize its recurrence. Also, the phenomenon is not alien to academia; hence, several types of research have been carried out in various fields of studies such as education, guidance and counseling, sociology, theology, and ethics.

The concern of this detailed deconstruction of marriage, divorce, and its unending impacts is a socioethical analysis of divorce as a major problem confronting children in the twenty-first century.

Divorce

With the years passing by, the cases of divorce in America are increasing at a rapid rate. Looking at history, the first-ever case of divorce happened in 1963 during American colonies presented in

Massachusetts at Puritan court. The statistics show that an increment in single-parent families is rapid since 1963.

The 1960s census data depicts that 9 percent of children were born in single-parent families, while in most of the cases, parents never get married, and most of them often get separated or divorced. In the last few decades, the percentage of born children in single-parent families has increased to 28 percent (McLanahan and Percheski, 2008).

Stephen Ruggles and Sheela Kennedy from the University of Minnesota have observed a decline in the divorce rate since 1980, and after the controlled changes in the age of people getting married, the rate of divorced couples has risen to 40 percent. It is because during the 1980s, the younger couple got married, and they have a high risk of getting a divorce (*The Washington Post*, 2017).

Even the population of African American in the United States also has a higher divorce rate. Farley and Allen (1987) and Cherlin (1992) mentioned that the statistics of married African American couple in the 1970s is 68 percent who were happily living their lives, but the percentage decreased to a tremendous rate.

Even the US Census Bureau in 2000 mentioned that an estimated percentage of married African American males is 16 percent as compared to White males with 60 percent. At the same time, there are Black females that are married up to 37 percent in comparison to White females with 57 percent (Harris and Bradley, 2004, p. 2).

The rate of divorce cases is increasing, and the laws administrating divorce cases have also changed with time. The judiciary court has made it essential to consider and support the child's authority, and alimony will be given to the reliable parent, and control must be given accordingly especially in fault-based divorces.

In most states, fault-based divorce legislation still exists, but according to the 1988 Family Support Act, no-fault divorce rules allow individuals to get a divorce without any proof. Even the bill was approved because of the increasing single parent who is usually mothers, and most of the mothers or fathers were unable to support the child or the basic needs (Peters 1986).

Thus, it is concluded that rates of divorce are increasing, and the rules and regulations administrating divorce are established, which are termed as a martial process. In the old days, elders consider divorce as an immoral act, and it was termed as a social shame especially when there are children involved in the divorce. Nowadays, divorce is a common event and may happen because of various reasons.

Most people perceive marriage as a contract instead of a commitment done in front of God. Women's entry into various fields of employment has indeed established a nonconventional opinion on marriage, or it can be said that conventional standards of marriage are overwhelming during modern times.

How many children are affected after a divorce? How does divorce influence the children's lives? How do divorce features worsen the consequences mainly for children? What are the features and effects observed in children after divorce? The paper examines the divorce effects on the well-being of children. It also depicts the behavior problems observed in children.

Even functionalists and different sociologists, including Talcott Parson, emphasize the stabilized social system that influences the value of every individual in the society. Every family must stay aware of roles assigned according to gender.

The men should focus on instrumental roles and offer financial support, while women should focus on expressive roles like taking care of the children and husband's emotional needs. If the family structure is stabilized, Parson states that it is a successful marriage (Parson and Bales, 1955, p. 315). Over the last few years, marital stability has decreased due to many factors.

Wolfers and Stevenson (2007) have seen economic gains among women and the technological revolution as the main reason for divorce. Women are now spending minimum time and concentration on household chores because great and advanced household appliances introduced in the market assist in decreasing the time spent on labor.

Dishwashers, dryers, and washers are exceptional products that increase productivity mainly in a home, enabling women to be a paramount part of the workforce. Women's entry into various fields of life has stressed marriage and leaves an adverse effect even on children's mindset regarding divorce.

Divorce directly affects the children's emotional and psychological well-being. Most of the kids, regardless of age, demand security, safety, trust, loyalty, and attention. After the process of divorce, every child goes through different experiences, while most of them go through psychological trauma.

According to the studies, it is clear that children with divorced parents develop antisocial behavior, depression, and anxiety along with aggressive and delinquent behavior. They do face abandonment and self-blame fears which behave as a contributing aspect in the divorce.

Every parent handles the process of divorce differently, and most of the feelings are diminished in a child. Even in the United States, almost millions of children experience cognitive, social harm after the parental divorce, leaving the kids vulnerable (Fagan and Churchill, 2012). Even Weiss mentions that divorce enables children to mature, and it changes the entire structure of the family, allowing kids to handle more responsibilities.

Furthermore, children attain more responsibility at an early age; it is because single parents are unable to pay for a babysitter, so children have to do chores or stay at home. Weiss argues about the concerns related to divorce, which involve various roles and responsibilities enabling children to be more practical and competent in social matters during teenage years. In the study, Weiss held the families accountable who have disabled children and demanded assistance or help during the divorce.

The customs and lifestyle of people in the Old Testament often seem peculiar and even harsh to modern readers. But from examples found in that book of Scripture, we still can learn much about proper relationships between husbands and wives and within families.

Old Testament stories illustrate well the point that everyone who comes into the Gospel comes out of his or her own culture. This lesson is important in our day as the church becomes established in nations with widely varying cultures and family traditions.

With all this diversity, it is impossible to conclude that the Gospel prescribes just one pattern of family life to suit all people in every culture and in every time. Certainly, Gospel principles remain universal, but their application in various cultures may differ.

We must be careful then not to rigidly base our views of family life for our time on family models in the Old Testament. There are however selected stories and counsel in the Old Testament that reach beyond Old Testament cultures and illustrate universal gospel principles.

SECTION 1

THE BIBLICAL PERSPECTIVE

CHAPTER 1

Marriage, Family, Divorce, and Biblical Perspective

In the last few decades, a wide-ranging and tremendous change has been observed in the Western family patterns. The phenomenal changes are increasing rapidly, which include divorce rates, enhanced out-of-wedlock births, and father absence because of globalization and same-sex marriages.

The cohabitation of individuals without a legal contract of marriage and civil unions is also the main cause of increased changes observed in Western family patterns (Browning, 2001:243). Nowadays, these Western societies are well-known as high-divorce societies.

Over the years, cohabiting couples are increasing since 1970, mainly in the United States, and the situation is increasing at a rapid rate even in Western societies. According to Gill (1997:81), many Christians have shown a great concern with a relevant observation that there has been a rapid decline observed in two-parent families but a rapid rise in teenage abortions and pregnancies, gay activism, and the spread of AIDS or HIV, and a broad confusion needs to be addressed regarding social limits and legal acts of obscenity and pornography.

In an article by Browning (2001:4), the modernization and globalization phenomena are well-documented because they both are termed as the roots of the disrupting forces in the patterns of a good family. Are these developments such as modernization regarded as normal or immoral cultural patterns in a society? Do these changes indicate a good family life, or do they term as a crisis?

The main purpose of the article is to mention the crucial principles of marriage, and the paramount ethical terms and norms are described below. The following are the necessary aspects:

- Heterosexual monogamous marriage is established by God. It is an exclusive, fashionable, or private relationship between a man and a woman (Douma, 1993:113). Polygamy was a norm or a tradition mentioned in Old Testament time, and it was practiced in by Lamech (Genesis 4:19), Esau (Genesis 26:34), and David, Solomon, and Abraham because monogamy was in a creational order.

  Polygamy is one of the descriptive issues discussed in detail in the historical events or lives of people, but the creational order is inflexible or termed as prescriptive. The principle establishes the base of marital relations in the New Testament (1 Chronicles 7:2, Ephesians 5:28–33, Colossians 3:19, and Titus 2:4).

  Although Polygamy does not need an introduction, it is described in detail but results in fall, while monogamy is inflexible and presented as prescriptive, or they are known as the will of God. The creational order eliminates the practice of same-sex marriages.

- The main objective of getting married is to get mutual guidance and seek mutual help (Ephesians 5:23–25), spiritual and physical fulfillment, and protection from immorality (1 Chronicles 7:1–7). According to Köstenberger (2004:98), reproduction process is also a paramount part of God's plan especially considered for married people.

  He refers, among other things, to Genesis 1:28, 9:1, and 35:11. Thus, this view faced many ethical issues because childless marriage is not considered inferior, and procreation holds secondary importance.

Marriage forms an intense relationship between a man and a woman on the physical and spiritual terrain. After marriage, husband and wife become one flesh because two individuals share lives in a dedicated and complete way because marriage is beyond sexuality. It is a deep and intense spiritual relationship between man, wife, and Christ (Ephesians 5:21–33).

It cannot be termed as a legal contract because it is a covenant before God between a man and a wife who indicates the covenant between God and his people (Douma 1993:114). Thus, marriage is entitled to be a sacred bond that is strengthened through intimacy, sacredness, mutuality, and exclusiveness (Köstenberger, 2004:91).

Children perceive the same human dignity and image because children's human dignity is based on their creation in God's image. The idea is the fundamental aspect of biblical faith to anthropology. Thus, this concept is summarized by Fedler (2006:83) with the conclusion that human beings hold good regard because human beings are created in the image of God.

The life of any human being is not disposable. Any human life must not be used to achieve its purposes because creation in the image of God depicts that human beings are created to spend fellowship with God and other noble human beings. Children share an equally high view of human beings as stated in Scripture.

The spiritual and godly base of marriage means that divorce is not liked by God, and it is against God's will. Moreover, divorce breaks the commitment and violates the promise of covenantal marriage character witnessed by other people and God (Brueggemann, 1997:452). It means divorce breaks the marriage vows.

According to religion, in the seventh commandment, God prohibits and prevents adultery, and the prohibition also involves the act of divorce. It is good to not think about every situation in a literalist manner because, concerning the seventh commandment and different parallel channels, divorce is provisioned in some circumstances.

The main reason for divorce as mentioned is when a man finds his wife indecent or inappropriate (Deuteronomy 24:1).

There has been fundamental equality concluded between man and his wife, and the provision is accountable to those wives who find their husband indecent and can seek divorce. The indecency term involves various acts of sexual immorality, and according to Jesus's teaching in the Sermon on the Mount it states that "it hath been said, whosoever shall put away his wife, let him give her a writing of divorcement: But I say unto you, That whosoever shall put away his wife, saving for the cause of fornication, causeth her to commit adultery: and whosoever shall marry her that is divorced committeth adultery" (Matthew 5:31–32 KJV).

Adultery means to break the spiritual and respectful relationship with God and other individuals (Bosman, 2004:274). It signifies the ethical and religious consequences and serves as a base for the termination of a marriage. There can be many other reasons for divorce, which can be collected from various biblical themes or are mentioned in the context of history.

Abandoning willfully is also a valid reason to file a divorce (1 Corinthians 7:15–16) because abandonment means breaking the promise of commitment and covenant. Another known reason to file a divorce is when the actions of the better half inhibit the other better half from staying loyal and sincere toward God (Acts 4:19–20).

It is important to have an ethical reflection on the passages that adultery does not lead directly to divorce. Methods of reconciliation and forgiveness assist in making the bond strong or are likely to be pursued. After forgiveness and repentance, remarriage can be considered. If forgiveness is not considered, according to the Scripture's teachings, the reconciliation laws will be dishonored.

Lastly, if any partner is addicted to drugs, alcohol, violence, psychopathy, sexual abuse, or constant humiliation, it will inhibit the relation of the partner with God, and divorce is accountable when other necessary remedies fail. Consequently, Douma (1996:275) has warned that divorce is regrettable and is termed as an extreme act.

In terms of marriage, many times, people say, "Behind every successful man, there is a good woman." A more accurate way to put this statement is that on the side of every successful man, there is a good woman. Your wife walks side by side with you, not behind because God didn't take a woman from the back of a man's spine. He took man and put him to sleep, and he made woman from his side, bone of his bone and flesh of his flesh, and made woman as a helpmate.

A woman is not to be behind her husband. She is to be on the side of her husband so that they can walk together side by side. Genesis 2:21 states, "God meat man to find deep sleep to create a woman."

CHAPTER 2

Biblical Dimensions on Divorce

The family is deeply embedded in the idea of the covenant. The formula of the covenant expressed in Genesis 17:7 describes the essence of this relationship (Rendtorff, 1998:11). God is the God of Israel and their descendants, and they will be his people. This covenantal relationship contains promises and instructions.

The covenant develops along familial lines. God promises his people that he will be their God but also the God of their children. The children are included in the covenant, and this inclusion is signified by circumcision. The promise of the covenant, sealed by the initiating rite of circumcision, addresses itself to the solidarity of the family unit (Palmer Robertson, 1980:152).

The children thus have a special status that requires special treatment. This idea is equally important in the New Testament dispensation as can be seen in Jesus's special concern for the children and the fact that baptism replaces circumcision as the sign of the covenant. The doctrine of salvation and especially the biblical view that children share fully in the salvation in Christ complement this idea.

Children are also justified by faith and receive the gift of faith just as much as adult believers. These gifts of grace are signified by the sacrament of baptism. In the theology of Paul, baptism is seen as the baptism in the death and resurrection of Christ (2 Corinthians 5:14–15) (Ridderbos, 1971:225).

Marriage and family are indispensable components of God's intention for fallen humanity. He carries redemption and renewal by way of his coming kingdom and the covenant with people and their children. Obedience to God encompasses the totality of the life of a believer. Therefore, the family should be seen as a sphere where the reign and authority of God should prevail.

The reign of Christ stretches to the deepest corners of this intimate social relation. Marriage and family life in Christian circles cannot be determined by nature or culture but only by the moral teachings of Scripture. Postmodern culture challenges this idea.

There is a tendency in Christian circles to condone modern customs regarding marriage and family and to relativize the distinctiveness of Christian morality. Gill (1997:86) detects and laments this tendency in the well-known 1995 report of the Church of England's Board for Social Responsibility (1995).

He warns against the "baptizing of a purely secular agenda." Still, he regards certain modern trends as not inherently sinful in terms of Christian virtues but "less than ideal." According to him, these are childlessness through spontaneous sterility, faithful cohabitation, and faithful homosexual relationships.

However, in my opinion, this "less than ideal approach" with respect to faithful cohabitation and homosexual relationships must eventually also lead to a "baptism of the secular" because it compromises the authority of God and the reign of Christ over marriage and family. It will introduce pragmatic, situation-oriented ethics that will, in the end, abolish Christian moral distinctiveness and pave the way for complete secularity.

To my mind, Christian churches today have the responsibility to proclaim the core values of marriage and family life and to protect this societal sphere even if it runs directly against the ethos of the new postmodernist worldview. To live according to the attitude of Christ means to be obedient to God.

In the family of God, relationships are characterized by equality. This observation corresponds with the implication of people being created in the image of God. Husband, wife, and children are essentially equal, and it is stated that children can escape the negative consequences of parental conflict when they are not caught in it by their parents; when their parents avoid direct, aggressive expressions of their conflict in front of them; or when they use compromise styles of conflict resolution.

Buchanan et al. (1991) found that with adolescents who were living part of the time with each parent, the effects of discord between parents were stronger, and they tended to feel caught in the middle. Children who were involved in their parent's disagreements and who felt they had to manage their parent's relationship to make things run smoothly were the most likely to feel depressed and exhibit deviant behavior (Buchanan, 1991).

Therefore, conflict *per se* is not necessarily the best predictor of adjustment and should perhaps not be used by itself as a sole determinant in making decisions about custody and access. Another major difficulty with using conflict as a determinant in custody and access decisions is that conflict almost invariably diminishes over time, and couples can move in and out of conflict both before and after separation and divorce.

In an examination of a number of common hypotheses relating to the effects of divorce on children, it found no support for the interparental hostility hypothesis. Instead, they suggest that when a number of stressors (i.e., economic deprivation, interparental hostilities, and the burden of single parenting) take their toll on custodial mothers, children fare less well.

However, when parents are psychologically able to provide a loving relationship, children will be buffered from the stresses divorce can engender and will prosper developmentally.

SECTION 2

THE SOCIAL PERSPECTIVE (THE WORLD)

CHAPTER 3

Trends of Divorces/Divorce Behaviors around the Globe

Divorce

With the years passing by, the cases of divorce in America are increasing at a rapid rate. Looking at history, the first-ever case of divorce happened in 1963 during American colonies presented in Massachusetts at Puritan court. The statistics show that an increment in single-parent families is rapid since 1963.

The 1960s census data depicts that 9 percent of children were born in single-parent families, while in most of the cases, parents never get married, and most of them often get separated or divorced. In the last few decades, the percentage of born children in single-parent families has increased to 28 percent (McLanahan and Percheski, 2008).

Stephen Ruggles and Sheela Kennedy from the University of Minnesota have observed a decline in the divorce rate since 1980, and after the controlled changes in the age of people getting married, the rate of divorced couples has risen to 40 percent. It is because during the 1980s, the younger couple got married, and they have a high risk of getting a divorce (*The Washington Post*, 2017).

Even the population of African American in the United States also has a higher divorce rate. Farley and Allen (1987) and Cherlin (1992) mentioned that the statistics of married African American couple in the 1970s is 68 percent who were happily living their lives, but the percentage decreased to a tremendous rate.

Even the US Census Bureau in 2000 mentioned that an estimated percentage of married African American males is 16 percent as compared to White males with 60 percent. At the same time, there are Black females that are married up to 37 percent in comparison to White females with 57 percent (Harris and Bradley, 2004, p. 2).

The rate of divorce cases is increasing, and the laws administrating divorce cases have also changed with time. The judiciary court has made it essential to consider and support the child's authority, and alimony will be given to the reliable parent, and control must be given accordingly especially in fault-based divorces.

In most states, the fault-based divorce legislation still exists, but according to the 1988 Family Support Act, no-fault divorce rules allow individuals to get a divorce without any proof. Even the bill was approved because of the increasing single parent who is usually mothers, and most of the mothers or fathers were unable to support the child or the basic needs (Peters 1986).

Thus, it is concluded that rates of divorce are increasing, and the rules and regulations administrating divorce are established, which are termed as a martial process. In the old days, elders consider divorce as an immoral act, and it was termed as a social shame especially when there are children involved in the divorce.

Nowadays, divorce is a common event and may happen because of various reasons. Most people perceive marriage as a contract instead of a commitment done in front of God. Women's entry into various fields of employment has indeed established a nonconventional opinion on marriage, or it can be said that conventional standards of marriage are overwhelming during modern times.

How many children are affected after a divorce? How does divorce influence the children's lives? How do divorce features worsen the consequences mainly for children? What are the features and effects observed in children after divorce? The paper examines the divorce effects on the well-being of children.

It also depicts the behavior problems observed in children. Even functionalists and different sociologists, including Talcott Parson, emphasize the stabilized social system that influences the value of every individual in the society. Every family must stay aware of roles assigned according to gender.

The men should focus on instrumental roles and offer financial support, while women should focus on expressive roles and taking care of the children and husband's emotional needs. If the family structure is stabilized, Parson states that it is a successful marriage (Parson and Bales, 1955, p. 315). Over the last few years, marital stability is decreased due to many factors.

Wolfers and Stevenson (2007) have seen economic gains among women and the technological revolution as the main reason for divorce. Women are now spending minimum time and concentration on household chores because great and advanced household appliances introduced in the market assist in decreasing the time spent on labor.

Dishwashers, dryers, and washers are exceptional products that increase productivity mainly in a home, enabling women to be a paramount part of the workforce. Women's entry into various fields of life has stressed marriage and leaves an adverse effect even on children's mindset regarding divorce.

Divorce directly affects the children's emotional and psychological well-being. Most of the kids, regardless of age, demand security, safety, trust, loyalty, and attention. After the process of divorce, every child goes through different experiences, while most of them go through psychological trauma.

According to the studies, it is clear that children with divorced parents develop antisocial behavior, depression, and anxiety along with aggressive and delinquent behavior. They do face abandonment and self-blame fears, which behave as a contributing aspect in the divorce.

Every parent handles the process of divorce differently, and most of the feelings are diminished in a child. Even in the United States, almost millions of children experience cognitive, social harm after the parental divorce, leaving the kids vulnerable (Fagan and Churchill, 2012). Even Weiss mentions that divorce enables children to mature, and it changes the entire structure of the family, allowing kids to handle more responsibilities.

Furthermore, children attain more responsibility at an early age; it is because single parents are unable to pay for a babysitter, so children have to do chores or stay at home. Weiss argues about the concerns related to divorce, which involves various roles and responsibilities enabling children to be more practical and competent in social matters during teenage years.

In the study, Weiss held the families accountable who have disabled children and demanded assistance or help during the divorce.

The customs and lifestyle of people in the Old Testament often seem peculiar and even harsh to modern readers. But from examples found in that book of Scripture, we still can learn much about proper relationships between husbands and wives and within families.

Old Testament stories illustrate well the point that everyone who comes into the Gospel comes out of his or her own culture. This lesson is important in our day as the church becomes established in nations with widely varying cultures and family traditions.

With all this diversity, it is impossible to conclude that the Gospel prescribes just one pattern of family life to suit all people in every culture and in every time. Certainly, Gospel principles remain universal, but their application in various cultures may differ.

We must be careful then not to rigidly base our views of family life for our time on family models in the Old Testament. There are however selected stories and counsel in the Old Testament that reach beyond Old Testament cultures and illustrate universal gospel principles.

Five Views of Marriage and Divorce

Marriage's patristic views and the opinion of early church fathers are highlighted by the Christian world until the sixteenth century. Many theologians outlined the church leaders' writings, and during the five centuries right after Christ, doctrinal positions are determined on many legal issues.

There is only one exception and unanimous in the Christ and Paul opinion, which taught individuals to suffer the hard luck of divorce because remarriage is not permitted irrespective of the cause.

Erasmian

Desiderius Erasmus is the theologian known in the sixteenth century: a fashionable contemporary of Martin Luther who uttered the latest position on remarriage and divorce. The remarriage and divorce opinion is broadly among the Protestant churches even today:

> It holds that Christ's words in Matthew 19:9 allowed divorce in the case of adultery and, since in Jewish marriage contracts the granting of divorce always implied the right to remarry, he also was permitting the innocent party to remarry.

Many people who own this opinion also have the rank that the majority of those who hold this view also takes the position that "Paul further expanded this concept by allowing divorce and remarriage in the case of the willing desertion on the part of the person's partner." Some people take the position to involve domestic violence, and the central theme is the position that seems perfect to remarry an innocent spouse.

Preterative

It was St. Augustine who presented his opinion and promoted Christ's answer to the Pharisees, "except for marital unfaithfulness," which passed over the question because some of them were frustrating and tried to hoax Him.

When he was found alone with his disciples, it was Christ who discovered the truth: Whoever divorces his wife and marries another woman commits adultery against her." Due to some reason, if a divorce happens, the position does not enable the remarriage of any spouse.

Betrothal

According to Christ's opinion, there is an "exception clause" for adultery in which it is allowed to break the engagement during the violation case of betrothal before marriage consummation. All the arguments are in favor of position and possess reliable merit.

It is good that an individual must understand the betrothal binding nature during the Christ, and recognition for a divorce needs to disrupt the engagement (as illustrated by Mary and Joseph in Matthew 1:10–20). One must need to understand that interpretation and clarification are possible.

The committed or engaged couples refer to their man as husband and woman as wife. Christ says not to discourse himself to the possibility, which opens misunderstanding ways and closes the door on canceling the engagement.

The point is clear that Christ must select the word carefully: *fornication* (*porneia*) to understand *adultery* (*moicheia*). It is good that both individuals speak about unfaithfulness in terms of adultery, premarital unfaithfulness, or marital faithfulness. Thus, the condition refers to the divorce before consummation and marriage, and both individuals can get married.

Consanguinity

It is a point of view termed as unlawful marriage doctrine. It occurs very rarely and often results in divorce, which is allowed only if both individuals are close relatives and married. According to some people, divorce is permitted if there is an only situation that refers to Christ's use of *porneia* involving sexual immorality.

According to the consanguinity point of view, divorce is recognized and instituted in many cases as unlawful marriages when most of the people consider it as a remarriage opposing Christ's and

Paul's teachings. In a lawful marriage, the divorced individual is not allowed to remarry, and the act of divorce is strictly forbidden.

Conclusion

When the research was started, I was sure to get definite and certain answers to many complex questions, which include, is marriage a covenant? And due to some reason, if yes, what is the implication to view marriage against the backdrop of the covenant? Is there any scriptural assistance to produce any type of marriage potentials? Is there any legislation that creates new marriage gradation?

All these questions are implicit, and most of the state representatives originated on a well-intentioned perception. Thus, covenant marriage is legal, and it is redundant because marriage is a covenant form. It is man who is unable to make marriage bond covenantal, and it can be weaker or stronger.

There is only one definite word that describes all types of holy union, which is *marriage*. It will simply remain holy and the complete description of a man and woman to join in front of God. Any fashionable term that tries to alter absoluteness is characteristic of all marriage that falls short. In an attempt to raise marriage, we have cheapened the other marriages, and precedent was passed.

It is assumed to pave the way for the creation of the hyphenated alternative toward the conventional marriage norms. The abrogation of God expressing commandments is disturbing because marriage is ultimate and binds all men and women every time.

Yes, indeed, God is the creator and is known as a covenant, and the divinely ordained union does not subject to any human or individual tinkering; he is the only creator of marriage and owns authority and capability to change nature. Instead of altering the institution, there exists a creation of both genders; let us attempt to understand the covenant, which is denoted by the great word *marriage*.

CHAPTER 4

The Dilemma of Divorce and the Growth of Teenage Girls

In general, divorce similarly affects teenage girls and boys, yet there are a few different ways that young boys and girls experience differently in an unusual way. Teenagers are affected by separation in some different manners than children.

A study shows that teenage girls, in general, have some negative manifestations such as anxiety, anger, and depression. These manifestations may disappear with time (Amato, 2001). For some people who are away from family problems, mothers have authority over their kids.

For teenage girls, research accompanies that building up a strong relationship with their mothers after the divorce encourages these girls to mend the burdens of divorce at a quicker speed than if they have stayed with their fathers. It's been discovered that the mother-girl relationship, in general, is quite tough to the anxieties of divorce. Circumstances surely vary in every household or situation (Størksen et al., 2006).

High divorce rates in the United States over the past twenty years have resulted in numerous changes in American family life with perhaps the most important consequences bearing on children whose families were disrupted; in 1970, 12 percent of American families with children under age eighteen were headed by single parents.

By 1984, one-fourth of American families and nearly 60 percent of Black families were headed by single parents (see Table 1). Millions of other children live in two-parent but reconstituted families, separated from at least one biological parent; in fact, Furstenberg, Nord, Peterson, and Zill's recent analysis (1983) indicates that less than two-thirds of American children live with both biological parents.

A number of studies use recent social and demographic trends to predict children's future living arrangements, and while these predictions vary, the consensus is that most youth will spend some time prior to age eighteen in a single-parent household (Bumpass, 1984, 1985; Furstenberg et al., 1983; Hofferth, 1985, 1986; Norton and Glick, 1986).

Hofferth (1985) suggests that the percentage of Black youth who will live with one parent for some period of time prior to age eighteen may be as high as 94 percent, while for White children, the corresponding figure is 70 percent. Norton and Glick's (1986) analysis yields a lower estimate but still projects that 60 percent of American children will live in a single-parent family before reaching age eighteen.

Various studies depict that separation can have a more-grounded negative effect on teenage girls, who will, in general, characterize themselves through relationships, association with others, and bonds with loved ones. At the point when the structure of their family, a structure they've known for the duration of their lives, is upset, an inside structure is likewise in danger of separating.

Teenage ladies will, in general, be associated with their mothers and will, in general, be more submissive and mindful than young men. In view of this, young ladies may hush up about their feelings. They may hide how they are truly feeling to watch out for their mother's acclimation to the change and show that everything is fine.

Despite the fact that they may hide their sentiments, adolescent girls could likewise have a postponed response to their feelings, which may later come on quietly. For example, a few teenage girls may feel disgrace, which can prompt low confidence and self-shame. This may likewise prompt looking for accomplices that don't treat them the manner in which they should be dealt with and having unfortunate relationships (Adam and Chase-Lansdale, 2002).

The literature shows that the solid connections a girl has with her parents can give a buffer to the separation. The relationship a girl has with her mother is critical. For a few, the mother-girl relationship endures after separation. Nonetheless, for the individuals who have a solid bond from the earliest point, that bond can fill in as a defensive factor during the split.

This is additionally valid for a female adolescent relationship with her father. Since most high school young girls favor their mothers during a separation, a youngster may have huge issues of trust on the off chance that she can't mend her relationship with her mother previously, during, or after a separation.

Recent studies give some new experiences into the impacts of divorce on the frequency and determination of teenage girls' danger practices. Specifically, teenagers of 12–18 years from such families were associated with hard-core drinking, alcohol intake, tobacco use, and cannabis use (to relax their minds) than the ones from married families.

Every one of these factors expanded as the teenagers became older. An important distinction was that the rates of alcohol consumption among children from both family types would in general meet over the long run, whereas the level of tobacco and marijuana usage in young ones from divorced families remained considerably elevated than those from complete families.

It was also found that the perseverance of the negative psychological impacts of separation was especially higher for teenage ladies (Wallerstein, 1991).

There is more mental illness and decreased prosperity in teen girls of divorced families; the explanation could be suffering clashes and issues in the family, e.g., in light of differences about care. There is the additional likelihood that teenage girls, to a bigger degree more than youthful kids, feel answerable for the decision of where to live and that this could speak to a wellspring of struggle with a corresponding decrease of mental change and prosperity.

The most grounded impact of separation in this investigation apparently is on scholastic issues. Such issues in kids after separation are frequently clarified by the absence of parental help and of a spotlight on school and schoolwork.

Clearly, when one parent is missing and the other parent has a much greater number of tasks and obligations as is regularly the situation, this can lessen scholarly consideration and backing to the adolescents especially the girls as they are sensitive creatures (Hines, 1997).

Research suggests that divorce can adversely influence the capabilities of young girls at educational and occupational levels. Tragically, almost 10 percent of young girls who have suffered a divorce have showed decreased interest to perform well in schools and colleges. Research also depicts that most young girls may do fine in studies and other tasks especially if they get help from one of their parents (Altonji et al., 2008).

The impacts of divorce can also alter the actual development cycle of teenage girls as the hormonal changes are related to their psychological well-being. One intriguing result is that young girls in divorced and second-time-married families show an earlier beginning of menstruation and physical development.

The majority of young girls are not usually mentally prepared for this earlier onset of puberty. Therefore, parents should be ready to discuss these subsequent changes early with their daughters so they may understand how to adapt to these changes on time than later.

In few teenage girls, the process of divorce causes them to feel like they have to mature quickly. A number of divorced parents struggle themselves with the influences of separation and need someone to look up to for help and assistance. Tragically, as a rule, these parents, particularly mothers, go to their daughters for this.

Many separated mothers depicted their girls as closest companions. They also believed they could easily talk to their daughters about anything, such as their own relationship flaws, depression, anxiousness, and monetary burdens.

Young children suffer a lot when a parent does not share individual issues with them as they would to a grown-up child. At the point when parents disclose an excess of their own problems, it is difficult for their teen girls at different levels (Kelly, 2000).

Therefore, it is concluded that divorce has a significantly negative impact on the psyche of teenage girls as they are more sensitive and close to their parents. They do not perform well in their social, academic, and professional life, appearing as mentally disturbed and extremely stressed. Their attitude toward people and life changes drastically under the critical circumstances encountered during the phase of separation.

CHAPTER 5

Dilemma of Divorce on Teenage Boys

Divorce has a major effect on the lives of family members especially children. Divorce represents the major social, physical, economic, and emotional loss in the lives of all family members, including adolescents and children. Teenage boys have a serious effect on their minds due to broken marriages. A distressing change is present in the life of children of all ages due to this effect.

Feelings of direct involvement in parents' life, losing emotional safety, change in lifestyles and defense, and many other unseen emotional distresses are present in a child's life due to the broken marriage. For all children, the divorce between parents is shocking as it trembles their dependence, lack of self-confidence, belief, and insecurity in them.

Divorce has a long-lasting effect. Family separation by getting divorced implies a huge death for both the baby. This leads to many psychological, mental, academic, and educational threats. Such psychosocial concerns in life are difficulties in private life, scholarly adaption, friend connection, success, health issues, and societal incompetence (Flach, 1980).

For instance, they may be compelled to live in a dramatic and traumatic loss of revenue and small accommodation in an environment with an elevated crime rate and poor-quality schools and protection, inadequate social security, and insufficient health services, and other subsidies.

The boys suffering from parents' divorce reveal more issues with behavior and mental and emotional well-being, reduced academic success, bad health, and social problems.

Also, the teenage boys of parents who are divorced are fairly unhappy with their teachers and parents as a response to feeling sad, educational issues, and mutual connection. In the absence of early-stage depressed mood, more were shown by the girls as opposed to male kids (Wauterickx, Gouwy, and Bracke, 2006).

Impact of Divorce on Teenage Boys

In teenage boys, there is a defensive aspect as according to the family education, they are more likely to respond to their parents' divorce with anger, delinquency, offensive life, and academic problems. They are always at risk of stroke, particularly if the dad is the parent with whom they no longer survive.

A theory states that it is the accumulation of stressful experiences that causes difficulties for boys (Kaye, 1989). There is just a little research that has tested this theory, but the findings seem to confirm it. Generally speaking, the more negative situation occurred after separation, the more trouble they may have.

There's also some fact that humans whose parents separate more than once are less well-off than boys whose parental separation is the only one they witness. The consequence for clinicians of this result is multiple. The majority of boys from divorced families, on the one hand, had no significant issues needing clinical assistance. But on the other hand, there were significant issues with a higher number of boys from separated families than within intact families (Kaye, 1989).

A further example to understand this is that there is no need for assistance for *most* kids in divorced families, but also more kids in this category than it was in intact families are expected to need some support. This is a dynamic one.

Different Stages

At any point during the divorce process, boys might be symptomatic, and these symptoms might even be the issue of therapy. In reality, with a push from a struggling teenage boy, those ex-spouses who manage to build a flexible and cooperative partnership always do so (Guinart and Grau, 2014).

Careful preseparation preparation can do much to enhance the effect of divorce on children, but the unavoidable upheaval at the time of divorce and the subsequent trial-and-error attempts to reconfigure the structure can serve as a trigger for boys' stage-related issues (Guinart and Grau, 2014).

Behavior Ratings

The teacher most informed about the boys at ages six and ten to fifteen years graded physical violence, resistance, irritability, carelessness, panic, and prosaic behavior using social behavior evaluation. Three items were tested for physical violence at ages six and ten to fifteen years: fighting with other children; kicking, biting, or hitting other children; and threatening or intimidating other children (Rydelius, 1983).

They do not exchange things, are grumpy and unfaithful, attack others, and are rude and disrespectful. The binary parameters of high irritability, high recklessness, severe anxiety, and high prosociality were built from these observations. Each one distinguishes boys in each of the respective sample distributions in approximately the upper quartile (Rydelius, 1983).

Feelings of Insecurity

Another specialist shows that individuals have the mentality that they'd be prepared to operate through it and fix any problems with their parents (Rosen, 1979). The children view parents who have given the children life as very capable individuals with extraordinary abilities to fulfill the children's needs. To manage for their parents, no topic should be too big (Rosen, 1979).

Feelings of Rejection

When the mother leaves the kids, they seem to become dismissed. But if the parent and someone else start another family, the emotions of failure may escalate ("Violent behavior in teenage boys has been traced to two factors-complications in delivery and maternal rejection," 1995).

I can remember fighting the feelings of hurt and rejection from my own childhood experience where my parents split after I was an adult and both of my parents begun new families with new partners (Spruijt and Duindam, 2005).

Feeling the Weight of Poverty

Because the income of the custodial parent decreases significantly, the sting of financial problems is 50 percent more likely for kids in broken homes to realize, which would lead to their feelings of shame, depression, and concern. It takes time to weigh the physiological, financial, and emotional ramifications of your breakup if you're seeking a divorce. On most occasions, in their divorced state, people get to know that they are not any happier.

Long-Term Effectiveness

Kids raised in divorced homes have several long-term negative influences. Some to consider are as follows:

1. More susceptible to misuse of drugs
2. Academically suffer
3. Durable mental pain triggered by depression and incapacity to participate in enduring new discussions
4. Social isolation, frustration, anxiety, and fear, which are also long-term implications.

Divorce plays a detrimental role in the lives of children. Among kids from divorced homes, behavior issues are normal. Boys appear to be more hostile toward others in general. Yet girls are still acting out. They are more likely to participate in sexual promiscuity or become parents of young people.

Christian Views on Divorce Effect on Teenage Boys

Long after the standardization of the Bible, they find their origin both in biblical references relating to the providing of the law to Joseph and political issues in the Christian world. Jesus stressed, according to the synoptic Gospels, the stability of marriage, as well as its dignity. Jesus says in the book of Matthew, "Moses authorized you to divorce your wives because of your hardness of heart, but it was not so from the beginning. And I tell you: whoever divorces his wife, except for extramarital sex."

Teenage boys also become very angry with one or both parents—abusive actions such as screaming can take the form of withdrawing from family communication. The boys would also take one parent's side and "penalize" the other with coercive conduct or by ignoring them directly.

To stay away from home, teenage boys will insist that they are supposed to spend more time with their friends, and if discouraged from doing so, they will become angry and violent. Teens might become less active in education, duties, and other activities. Grades will also decrease, and a marked rise in truancy can be observed.

Conclusion

Two types of analyses, the characteristics of the parents and the boy, were examined. Low educational achievement, first becoming a parent as a child, low socioeconomic status (SES), and divorce were the parental characteristics just before the boy's sixth birthday. Each of these is expected to raise the likelihood of a child's involvement in the two high trajectories of physical violence relative to the two lower-level classes based on prior studies.

All parental side effects have been reported before the birth of the boy except perhaps the separation and breakup parameters. It is difficult to ascertain if their correlation with the actions of the boy is due to genetic factors or environmental conditions since biologically insightful knowledge was not available.

Boys at the age of twelve to thirteen years that belong to divorced families indulge in drug abuse, alcohol abuse, tobacco use, and marijuana use. For both male and female teenagers from both divorced and married families, the level of involvement in binge drinking, alcohol use, tobacco usage, and marijuana use increased by age.

The effects of domestic violence on smoking use and drug use were consistent for boys (Golombok, 1984). For males or females, there was no impact of divorce on hard drug use. Divorce children's study and clinical work focused mainly on the family breakdown as a stressful occurrence and its impact as a crisis on children (Golombok, 1984).

Based on clinical experience, the next section of the book will consider the children's possible long-term issues in key developmental areas, managing frustration and violence, disconnection, and gender identity. Implications are raised for mitigation and service provision. So we conclude that divorce has a dangerous effect on teenagers.

SECTION 3

THE PSYCHOLOGICAL PERSPECTIVE

CHAPTER 6

Declining Institution of Marriage

The foundation of marriage is weak nowadays, and globally, the establishment of union is significantly less. According to statistics, a significant decline in marriage is observed during the last two decades. There is a rapid decrement of almost 50 percent in British society regarding marriages, and it is likely to be most affected by the phenomenon.

The weak establishment of marriage is because of many reasons involving the wedding costs and expenses, the culture evolution, and the rise of cohabitation. Nations all over the world are well aware of the rising issue and playing a controversial role. The essay demonstrates the associated factors of the decline and the actions, which are the paramount reason for marriage decline.

Marriage is considered an obsolete and outdated establishment. It forms a bond between two people of different genders usually. Both of the people try their best to develop better facilities for various reasons including love, but still, they have to go through many challenges.

In marriage, both persons have to manage responsibilities accordingly, and the good times are counted due to money, while serious affairs, issues, and family troubles are a part of marriage. Marriage is also termed an outdated institution. The successor community and society have taken serious measures to repair the structure but are not succeeding in revolutionizing its template.

Thus, there is an urge by the subconscious mind to beat the beaten system a very long time ago. Society perceives marriage institutions entirely differently, but according to social anthropologist Darwin, he has not found anything unnatural or unusual in getting married.

A valid foundation is based on the principle of Darwin, while Ridley demonstrates a dishonorable debate regarding getting married. He mentions that getting into a relationship or in a bond of marriage is not a facility to get a child, but it can be believed to raise a child facility.

The book here explored the underlying perceptions that getting married is important and why still the rate of marriages is decreasing in our society. The next article mentions how the marriage system will work in the developed countries. But for many smart and obvious people, protecting marriage is not the ultimate reason.

The idea still regulates among many people that marriage is obsolete, unnecessary, unnatural and will surely fail. There are many reasons due to which it is worth fighting, so we have proposed an ultimate solution to eliminate the marital crisis in the modern world. We have also mentioned the main and common criticisms.

Marriage is known as a monogamy system that evolved because of rapid advancement. One of the great and outstanding aspects of marriage is its universality. Every nation and main civilization follow specific norms for a reliable marriage system. Even in human society or in the jungle, marriage aims to offer the main benefits to everyone.

Firstly, marriage offers a great opportunity for women and men to raise intelligent children. Secondly, it allows the couple to develop a good sense of accomplishment, which is not achieved with the involvement of other humans. Lastly, marriage lays a stable impact on human society and assists to improve the living lifestyle of people.

The Issue of Choice and the Changing Decade

In the last some decades, it is assumed that everyone will get married, give birth to babies, and live in a white-picket-fence house. Since childhood, the concept of getting married is engrained in our minds, but the idea is not innovative enough to appeal to younger generation.

The choice of getting married is entirely theirs, not just the parents, grandmothers, aunts, and the society keeps on reminding them that it is the right time to get married. The younger generation finds it a powerful choice to get married.

The pressures and losing one's identity that comes with getting married are another overpowering thought that is restraining the acceptance of this lifelong bond. Being an independent individual, you may think marriage is all about give-and-take, but most people do not want to let go of their independence and participate equally.

Such people do not need to get married because it does not work until unless both the man and the woman participate equally. There are times when women do not feel well and do not have the energy to prepare dinner, attend the man and woman or friends and family, or attend in social functions.

As the last blog states, the reasons for divorce and marriage are not a written agreement, but every way of life will be changed dynamically. And when kids are born, autonomy is shred. The younger generation is nowadays fast and prefers to live their life instead of being bogged down by a life partner.

The honeymoon phase is considered to be the beautiful phase, but when the phase is over, reality soon hits the minds, and the couple realizes that they haven't signed life for all of this.

Marrying for the Sake Of Marrying

When we feel we have the right person to settle with, we go for marriage right away, but it is termed as a doomed situation. The experts say that anyone can never settle with someone right or good enough in marriage because marriage is a lifetime contract of partnership.

No one can have a good-enough person to get settled for life because time is optimal to date with the person for several years. Obviously, after marriage, you will see yourself as a well-settled person, but marriage is not what you perceive, and the two people will change each other's destiny for their entire life.

There are still too many gender roles in a marriage, which is a common perception that has overwhelmed people with the rise of feminist movements around the world. You may have observed that Cinderella even ran away instead of putting on her slipper. Women expect a lot in married life. They expect the parents aspects, laundry, grocery shopping, cleaning, and cooking.

Moreover, most women are working women, enabling them to handle and manage a lot of work, so before getting the idea to get married, make sure you know and stay clear how the life partner needs to break and let go of gender roles, and they also manage household work. Yes, of course, men can handle a lot of household work.

Working Women, Single Women

After the feminist movement, women are participating and working as permanent members of various organizations. They are trying hard to deal with their career instead of being typical housewives or moms who stay at home. Such women need to be rewarded, who handle kids and manage their office work as well. It is not okay to ask your spouse about the job and career because no one can stop you from achieving your goals just because you are a new Mrs. X.

Having kids out of wedlock is no longer seen as the taboo that it was. Couples can adopt a child, conceive, or raise the child together while ignoring the traditional aspects of marriage. It is good that the young generation does not care about others and no longer gives importance to what people will say and whether they are opting for a child or else.

The Need for Freedom

In married life, freedom is necessary for both man and woman to pursue hobbies, interests, and social engagement, enabling an individual partner to enjoy their own space. Many couples are not compatible, and it is observed that they do not prefer to get married for the sake of this. Being single and getting around the old married couples, a lot of hostility, emotions, blame, and other motions are observed; even most of the couples in the start of their forties behave like old couples.

Marriage is indeed beautiful, and sharing life with the best partner feels amazing. There are two trends in getting married, marrying and blaming or regretting the decision, and then the young generation do not prefer to get a government job, and a wedding in a five-star hotel shows that both man and woman are soul mates.

If you are in love, chances are that you will stay happy with your partner. It is good to have meaningful long talks, and talk with your spouse about responsibilities, goals, keeping the identity, deal breakers, and even the China pattern. A marriage must be done right and will stay forever.

The Class-Based Decline in Marriage

According to statistics, half of the adults, around 52 percent, were married in 20008, and in 1960, it was 72 percent. The decline in marriages is because of the class line. Almost a 16 percent point gap was observed in the marriage rate between children whose parents have divorced and those who have not received diploma, or less is 48 percent and graduates 64 percent.

The gap percentage in 1960 was 72 percent and 76 percent. The survey concludes that people with high school diplomas do not want to get married, but the college graduates with financial stability do get marry with a percentage of 38 percent.

Is Marriage Becoming Obsolete?

According to the survey, 39 percent of people say that marriage is a traditional and outdated system. The same question was asked in 1978, and 28 percent of people voted yes. Sixty-two percent of people were a part of the traditional phenomenon, while 42 percent of people were troubled by getting married.

Americans indeed stay concerned about the family's future and marriage because 67 percent of adults are optimistic and the other 50 percent are concerned about the educational system of the country. Forty-six percent show interest in the economic system of the country, while others that deal in ethics and morals are up to 41 percent because of being conservative. The uncertainties are growing at a rapid rate.

An Ambivalent Public

The public's response to changing marital norms and family forms reflects a mix of acceptance and unease. On the troubled side of the ledger, seven in ten (69 percent) say that the trend toward more single women having children is bad for society, and 61 percent say that a child needs both a mother and father to grow up happily.

On the more accepting side, only the minority says that the trends toward more cohabitation without marriage (43%), more unmarried couples raising children (43%), more gay couples raising children (43%), and more people of different races marrying (14%) are bad for society. Relatively few say that any of these trends are good for society, but many say that they make little difference.

Group Differences

Where people stand on the various changes in marriage and family life depends to some degree on who they are and how they live. The young are more accepting than the old of the emerging arrangements; the seculars are more accepting than the religious; liberals are more accepting than conservatives; the unmarried are more accepting than the married, and in most cases, Blacks are more accepting than Whites.

The net result of all these group differences is a nearly even three-way split among the full public. A third (34 percent) say that the growing variety of family arrangements is a good thing; 29 percent say that it is a bad thing, and 32 percent say that it makes little or no difference.

The Resilience of Families

The decline of marriage has not knocked family life off its pedestal. Three-quarters of all adults (76 percent) say that their family is the most important element of their life; 75 percent say that they are "very satisfied" with their family life, and more than eight in ten say that the family they live in now is as close as (45 percent) or closer than (40 percent) the family in which they grew up. However, on all these questions, married adults give more positive responses than unmarried adults do.

The Definition of Family

By emphatic margins, the public does not see marriage as the only path to family formation. Fully, 86 percent say that a single parent and child constitute a family; nearly as many (80 percent) say that an unmarried couple living together with a child is a family, and 63 percent say a gay or lesbian couple raising a child is a family.

The presence of children clearly matters in these definitions. If a cohabiting couple has no children, a majority of the public says that they are not a family. Marriage matters too. If a childless couple is married, 88 percent consider them to be a family.

The Ties That Bind

In response to a question about whom they would assist with money or caregiving in a time of need, Americans express a greater sense of obligation toward relatives—including relatives by way of fractured marriage—than toward best friends. The ranking of relatives aligns in a predictable hierarchy.

More survey respondents express an obligation to help out a parent (83 percent would feel very obligated) or grown child (77 percent) than say the same about a stepparent (55 percent) or a stepsibling or half-sib (43 percent). But when asked about one's best friend, just 39 percent say that they would feel a similar sense of obligation.

Changing Spousal Roles

In the past fifty years, women have reached near parity with men as a share of the workforce and have begun to outpace men in educational attainment. About six in ten wives work today, nearly double the share in 1960.

There's an unresolved tension in the public's response to these changes. More than six in ten (62 percent) survey respondents endorse the modern marriage in which the husband and wife both work and both take care of the household and children; this is up from 48 percent in 1977.

Even so, the public hasn't entirely discarded the traditional male-breadwinner template for marriage. Some 67 percent of survey respondents say that in order to be ready for marriage, it's very important for a man to be able to support his family financially; just 33 percent say the same about a woman.

The Rise of Cohabitation

As marriage has declined, cohabitation (or living together as unmarried men and women) has become more widespread, nearly doubling since 1990, according to the Census Bureau. In the Pew Research survey, 44 percent of all adults (and more than half of all adults ages thirty to forty-nine) say that they have cohabited at some point in their lives. Among those who have done so, about two-thirds (64 percent) say that they thought of this living arrangement as a step toward marriage.

The Impact on Children

The share of births to unmarried women has risen dramatically over the past half-century, from 5 percent in 1960 to 41 percent in 2008. There are notable differences by race: Among Black women giving birth in 2008, 72 percent were unmarried.

This compares with 53 percent of Hispanic women giving birth and 29 percent of White women. Overall, the share of children raised by a single parent is not as high as the share born to an unwed mother, but it too has risen sharply—to 25 percent in 2008, up from 9 percent in 1960.

The public believes children of single parents face more challenges than other children—38 percent say that they face "a lot more" challenges, and another 40 percent say that they face "a few more" challenges. Survey respondents see even more challenges for children of gay and lesbian couples (51 percent say that they face a lot more challenges) and children of divorce (42 percent say that they face a lot more challenges).

In Marriage, Love Trumps Money

Far more married adults say that love (93 percent), making a lifelong commitment (87 percent), and companionship (81 percent) are very important reasons to get married than say the same about having children (59 percent) or financial stability (31 percent). Unmarried adults order these items the same way. However, when asked if they agree that there is "only one true love" for every person, fewer than three in ten (28 percent) survey respondents say, "I do."

CHAPTER 7

Psychological Impact of Divorce on Children under the Age of Eighteen

When a couple decides to terminate the marital union, "Divorce" happens to impact kids' lives, snatching their identities and making them suffer from emotional and psychological trauma. Divorce had an awful psychological impact on age eighteen children as some of them start considering themselves the reason, become angry, and opt aggressive behavior; being separated from mother/father divides them into two pieces, so each situation is unique from another. That is the "cruel reality."

Divorce is a stress indicator that badly influences the life of kids, targeting their emotional health and distinguishing them from other kids of their ages. Especially, females deal with more psychological issues and problems that destroy their interpersonal relationships and personal life (Huurre T., Junkkari H., and Aro H. 2006).

According to the National Institute of Child Health and Human Development, the most vital topic to cope up for a healthy generation is divorce. Divorce had a long-term negative impact on children's mental health throughout their lives, making them strange and odd in behavior and approaches as the aftermath of divorce involves them into severe emotional disorders (Chase-Lansdale P. L., Cherlin A. J., and Kiernan K. E., 1995).

All around the globe, different countries face an increase in divorce rates, significantly affecting Maldives and the United States.

Demo D. and Acock A. argue in *Journal of Marriage and Family* that the high divorce rate in the United States over the past few years has resulted in changes in the American family life system and status, disturbing millions of children separated from one of their biological parents.

Less than two-third of American children live with their family. Thus, those who are away from their parents face anxiety and depression attacks. Jacobson D. S. argued that children after separation/divorce need their father's encouragement the most. Being away from him for that, he observed thirty families and activities lost after parents' divorce. That finding indicates that kids start missing their father in the first year of their parent's separation.

Divorce is a susceptible situation where partners need to decide about kids and their future. Children under age eighteen feel more like a burden for their parents. That indulges them more in depression and anxiety as children today face many challenging encounters, including how to maintain school and deal with specific peer pressures that arise.

Kids are dealing with even stricter decisions at a much younger age regarding increased family pressures, society and socioeconomic strains, and academic stressors. The divorced ratio is touching high up to the sky. That shows increased numbers of children are being raised in divorced households. Today, fifty to sixty percent of all children will live in a single-parent home (Jeynes, 2002).

Moreover, now parents are so busy that they cannot manage time, and after divorcing their partner, life changes and goes on in another domain where it seems complicated to manage as a parent; thus, it is where the child takes the first step toward negative approaches.

So disorder in children's lives starts when it seems impossible to hold. Some of this disruption may occur immediately and be very apparent, and some may lie underground, rotting, only to rise and disturb children later even after they have become adults.

Here are some important questions to ponder: What are the impacts that divorce has on elementary-aged children move concurring to diverse components? Does family structure itself expect to only affect the levels of uneasiness in children from isolated families? Within the occasion, what are other contributing factors that will affect children from isolated families? And most importantly, why did the divorce rate increase over the period, and how does it make children depressed?

Various approaches suggest that social values, socioeconomic reasons, work-related stress, and family pressure sum up into divorce and torn happy family due to which children of growing age have no role model to follow nor no one to guide; instead, they remain confused on whom to rely on.

Such children have faced uneasiness among children of their age. The degree, length, and impacts of the effect are wide. As detailed by Wyman, Cowen, Hightower, and Pedro-Carroll (1985), person contrasts, characteristics of the child, situational components, and accessibility of assets played a noteworthy part in a child's alterations to separate.

Parents' Divorce versus Children

Children under age eighteen agonize during the divorce of their parents. Families should be cognizant of the gender roles that are appointed to them upon development. While men take on the "instrumental role," delivering financial support, women take up the "expressive role," confirming that the emotional needs of the children and the husband are met.

That's when a marriage is settled and structured. But with the passage of time, these approaches are changed and transformed into intermingle situation where both partners try to manage in the start and later end it up being separate or divorced with the mutual consensus that has an adverse impression on how children observe divorce and can have philosophical effects on their psychological and emotional well-being.

Parents' Divorce versus Children's Social Development

Studies have shown that children often have an upsurge in anti-social behavior, anxiety, and depression, along with increased criminal and aggressive behavior due to parent's divorce. When social development is discussed, nature and nurture are some of the key disputes in child development as a child's improvement is affected by hereditary fabric (nature) and how much is decided by natural impacts like environment and surroundings (nurture).

In terms of social development, a child is born to be a determinant of being an explorer or silent observer on which he/she decide how to opt for changes.

Parents' Divorce versus Psychological Theories

Different psychologists have concluded that there's a relationship between three specific theories to clarify the relationship between the child's age at the time of divorce and the psychosocial change.

The *critical theory* is the fundamental organized theory that concludes that the impacts of divorce on children move as a work of the developmental challenges stood up to by the child at different stages in his or her enhancement. At the age of three to five, it's the worst time of divorce as it lies awful impacts on children.

The second theory, which is the *cumulative effect hypothesis*, states that the influence of divorce upon children is understood from the time the divorce ensues and throughout the life expectancy of the child. With the beginning of divorce, there will be a bigger rise of influences for the child.

The third theory, *recency theory*, encapsulates the fact that divorce is stressful at any period of the life cycle of the child. The possessions of separation are short-lived, and children tend to recover completely within a year or two, according to this theory.

Negative Impacts

Children who faced their parents' divorce as the biggest tragedy in life have negative impacts. Some of those are given below:

- They face relationship struggles later in life.
- They have a trust issue with a partner.

- They involve risky behaviors.
- Depression is the main pillar throughout their lives.
- They are aggressive and rude in nature.
- Deals with feeling of rejection.

Children not counseled of the division, in any case, ought to bear the insane ride, causing inconvenience for the complete family. Investigation illustrates that partition makes hurt adolescence from which they can never recover.

Effective Parenting

Parents go to communicate effectively with their children, openly communicating adore and do commitment. In this way, children get it that it is typical to have numerous sentiments about their separation or division.

Researchers and Their Viewpoints Regarding the Psychological Impact of Divorce on Children under Eighteen

Rogers F. and Judkis J. (1996) elaborate that divorce causes a massive interruption in children's lives. Some of this interference may occur instantly and be very apparent, and some may lie underground, rotting, only to rise and affect children later even after they have become adults, while Rogers (1996) further elaborates that the family-structure disruption caused by a divorce affects everyone involved especially the children.

Elementary-aged children involved in a disturbance in their family structure due to a divorce may experience more increased levels of anxiety in comparison with their counterparts from intact two-parented homes. Divorce is that indicator that badly influences the life of kids, targeting their emotional health and making them what they are not so that mothers are often granted custody while fathers are granted just visit (Huurre T., Junkkari H., and Aro H. 2006).

How to Handle the Situation if Children Are
Facing Hard Time in Recovering

Don't lie to your children by telling fake stories, and don't pressurize your children in the middle, and don't ask them where to live and with whom to live. Most importantly, don't ever say that your divorce is because of them or you fall apart because of any issue. This will make them low and will make their self-esteem more or less zero.

CHAPTER 8

Impacts of Divorce on Cognitive, Social, and Psychological Growth of under Eighteen

The world is a fast-paced, developed zone with adversities and different cultural traditions. People are fond of many ethnicities and cultures, but there are many fundamental changes on similar ground levels. This shows the connectivity between humans and the relativity of going through similar human behaviors.

Divorce is one of the most debatable aspects of life, which, in some cases, is good, and in some, it works as a toxic one for the psychological, social, and cognitive approaches of children. Divorce, in the literal meaning, is separation or legally dissolving one's marriage contract. Divorce is the most challenging decision taken by both partners especially when children are involved.

Divorce means children lost contact with one of their parents especially their father. That makes them less attached to their father; it can be incredibly hard, but if both parents strive to work together to make it for their children, even postdivorce, relations can live with care, but unfortunately, the chances of this condition are rare as effects of parent's separation have long-lasting impacts.

Emily Doskow, in her book *Nolo's Essential Guide to Divorce*, states, "Divorce is one of the most stressful life events anyone goes through."

According to the Pew Research Center, about 40 percent of new marriages in the United States in 2013 included one spouse who had been married before, and in 20 percent of new marriages, both spouses had been married before.

Every year, millions of children under age eighteen experienced the divorce of their parents. Single parents failed to handle their children, or sometimes, due to lack of interaction and communication, the child suffers emotionally, psychologically, and socially; adopts unsuitable sex roles; has lost concentration in education; becomes delinquent and depressive; develops attitudinal and behavioral glitches, drug and alcohol addiction, and antisocial approaches in his or her life; and always tries to compare his/her single parent with two-parent families.

Divorce creates unconstructiveness in parents, and their children relation, among them mother-son relationship, suffers the most as mothers try to be more restraining by giving inappropriate orders and show aggressive behavior, playing both parents' role. That is the main hurdle in children progress throughout their life (Levitin T. E., 1979).

Social Impact of Divorce on Children under Age Eighteen

Antisocial behavior includes low intelligence, low school accomplishment, child physical abuse, parental dispute, cold parental attitude, disrupted families, low-size family income, peer differences, criminal pressure, and dependency. Without both parents' guidance and love, children become quite preferable to spend time alone rather than being in any group or with friends.

Children under eighteen become violent and anticommunal, lose their temper, show no hesitation in assailing someone, show increase disobeying intensity and aggression build in their behaviors, lose social life interest, and go through problems with peers that often consider them as weak and having a fear of rejection from them that makes them socially distanced from everyone around them.

Moreover, these issues arise with the passage of time if single parents are doing full-time jobs for running household responsibilities and children. Cooking, dusting, cleaning, and washing clothes are often assigned to children as household duties that often overload them to be away from social activities and interactions if they are too young to manage.

Antisocial children are often depicted as disobedient, bossy, bully, unmanageable, and hyper as they often go through questions like, why did your mother leave your father? Why don't your mother and father live together anymore? Do you enjoy life like other kids? How often do you visit your mother/father? Do your single parents have bf? Are your single parents living with you?

Tooley K. (1976) states, "The children whose behavior is extreme and whose environment seems to offer no hope for controlling or modifying their behavior are treated as inpatients." In frustration and anxiety, children start alcohol and drug consumption to make themselves stress-free that further attacks their mental health.

Different studies have shown that children who have gone through divorce of their parents before age eighteen witness social withdrawal more and try to accommodate themselves in following the corrupt directions of society. Parents' divorce for children in adulthood or young age worked as a chain reaction that does not determine how it will echo over the years as its impacts are more than anyone can ever think of.

Psychological and Cognitive Impact of Divorce
on Children under Age Eighteen

Divorce had short-term or long-term impacts on children. Short-term effect of divorce on children under eighteen is anxiety, constant stress, mood swings, sadness, and disillusion, while long-term effect of divorce varies from these behavioral and social problems: trouble with a relationship, drug abuse, higher rates of being involved in sexual activities, depression, socioeconomic problems, and antisocial nature-nurture in them. Children under eighteen go through severe psychological impacts throughout their life span.

Different psychologists research on it and found out that more divorced rates are observed in families where children have experienced parent's divorce during their early childhood as they can't understand and depend on partner relationship, which clearly depicts lack of trust and dependency.

Divorce is stressful and toxic for children. Due to long-term useless feelings and stress, children plunge into depression that becomes impossible to handle if not treated on time. The major psychological trauma that children go through is the missing factor of the father from their lives as mothers are often allowed custody while fathers can visit their child once a month.

Boys under eighteen missed outdoor activities and bonds with their fathers; moreover, without fathers, they fell prey to negative energies and people of society, while girls under eighteen need father's love and support throughout their life.

After divorce, the postseparation behavior of parents toward their kids affects their mental health more, making it difficult for them to adjust at school and with family, friends, and their own selves. Divorce had a long-term negative impact on children's mental health throughout their lives, making them strange and odd in behavior and approaches as the aftermath of divorce causes them severe emotional disorders (Chase-Lansdale et al., 1995).

Children who frequently hear pessimistic remarks from one parent about the opposite may suffer distractions in parental affection and feel pressured to declare loyalty to at least one parent or another or both. Few specific qualities have been related to strength and capacity, including a nice personality and normal or higher intellectual capacities in children who faced psychological tiredness because of parents' divorce as compared to those who did not.

Kids invested with positive attributes are better ready to search out and uphold from others and to adjust to change, though youngsters with troublesome dispositions or troublesome conduct are bound to battle to adjust in the outcome of separation.

Children under age eighteen suffer during the separation of their parents. Research has shown that divorce has a more harsh impact on cognitive and psychological approaches of children aged five to ten years in comparison to those who live with both of their parents, whereas older children above age ten till eighteen whose parents separated were more liable to struggle educationally than their peers whose parents stayed married.

Their mental health, cognitive approaches, psychological values, and emotional attachments are all different from each other. Teenagers also cope with many poignant symptoms alternating from fury to fear, loneliness to depression, and guilt to anxiety.

Many youngsters have a hard time accepting the divorce on which Gillian Flynn quotes this in a magnificent piece of writing, "My dad had limitations. That's what my good-hearted mom always told us. He had limitations, but he meant no harm. It was kind of her to say, but he did do harm."

Lisa Barron (2010) argued that if children are in the custody of their mother, then enduring a strong relationship with the father or noncustodial parent is crucial for keeping children psychologically connected to both parents. Regrettably, noncustodial parents have been shown to have little contact with their children after a divorce has occurred.

To comprehend the connection, psychological bonding is so important during the earliest years of a child's life and endless years of adulthood when problems may carry into middle age maladjustment. After divorce, parents should teach their children how to live openly and wholeheartedly with normal living standards, the way they were doing earlier before their parent's divorce, to make it work in contrast to their good psychological health as C. JoyBell C. quoted:

> There is no such thing as a "broken family." Family is family and is not determined by marriage certificates, divorce papers, and adoption documents. Families are made in the heart. The only time family becomes null is when those ties in the heart are cut. If you cut those ties, those people are not your family. If you make those ties, those people are your family. And if you hate those ties, those people will still be your family because whatever you hate will always be with you.

Shinn M. (1978) claimed that financial hardship, high levels of anxiety, and low levels of parent-child communication are causes of poor performance among children in single-parent families. Parents who split are less likely to devote themselves to their children while together; instead, they choose separation to protect their children from the effects of conjugal conflict.

The major trauma that children face is that they consider a two-parent family best as compared to their single-parent family. They always go through difficulties in ascertaining parents who divorced would have been well off having the parents remained together for his/her as the child wants them to be a happy family, not to be separated as divorce is demonstrated as an individually enforceable choice.

Divorce allows mothers to protect their children from disputes but prohibits joint time spent by parents with their children. Mental health problems, antisocial behavior, anxiety, depression, insecureness, disobedience, drug and alcohol addiction, behavioral issues, and stress make children suffer throughout their educational, personal, and professional life.

In their life span, under-eighteen children go through tragic happenings; as a young child, they don't understand why they need to struggle and visit two homes and why their parents are not living together. Being teenagers, they consider divorce as their fault, react aggressively, and try to avoid meeting their parents.

In the end, families should be aware of the gender roles when marriage is settling between two people and that men take on the "instrumental role," bringing fiscal support, managing all terms of outside house chores, and being the bread earner of the family who is there to make decisions and to guide the family. If the wife or child complains, it's his duty to let them talk their viewpoint and resolve their issues.

Women take up the "expressive role," confirming that the emotional needs of the children and the husband are met, taking care of the family, managing the household, dealing with children's behavior, and making them learn and interact regarding life and all values of lives.

But as we are living in a revolutionary span where these approaches are altered and distorted into an amalgamate situation where both partners try to manage in the start and later end up being separated or divorced with the mutual consensus as they can't find adjustment or don't try to adjust with each other, both of them want to rule the family, and both are working professionals that make it tough for their personal lives, it has an adverse impression on how children observe divorce and can have effects on their psychological and emotional well-being.

Parents are so busy that they cannot manage time, and after a divorce, life changes and goes on in another sphere where it seems complicated to get it done as a parent, so the child takes the first step toward negative approaches.

Parents need to counsel their children before and after their divorce, manage time once in a week where both of them are with their kids, and have a family get-together or picnic so that their child will be attached to them, as well as for happiness and peace of the family that is no more together physically but attached with soul and heart.

REFERENCES

Adam, E. K., & Chase-Lansdale, P. L. 2002. "Home sweet home(s): parental separations, residential moves, and adjustment problems in low-income adolescent girls." *Developmental psychology*, *38*(5), 792.

Altonji, J. G., Elder, T. E., & Taber, C. R. 2008. "Using Selection on Observed Variables to Assess Bias from Unobservables When Evaluating Swan-Ganz Catheterization." *American Economic Review*, *98*(2), 345–50.

Amato, P. R. 2001. "Children of divorce in the 1990s: an update of the Amato and Keith (1991) meta-analysis." *Journal of family psychology*, *15*(3), 355.

Barron, Lisa. 2010. "Divorce and it's side effects on the development of children."

Chase-Lansdale, P. L., Cherlin, A. J., & Kiernan, K. E. 1995. "The long-term effects of parental divorce on the mental health of young adults: A developmental perspective." *Child development*, *66*(6), 1614–1634.

Demo, D. H., & Acock, A. C. 1988. "The Impact of Divorce on Children." *Journal of Marriage and the Family*.

Demo, D., & Acock, A. 1988. "The Impact of Divorce on Children." *Journal of Marriage and Family*, *50*(3), 619–648. doi:10.2307/352634.

Flach, F. 1980. "Introduction: Divorce and the Psychiatrist." *Psychiatric Annals*, *10*(4), 11–11. DOI: 10.3928/0048-5713-19800401-05.

Golombok, S. 1984. "Child custody: A study of families after divorce." *Behaviour Research And Therapy*, *22*(1), 97–98. DOI: 10.1016/0005-7967(84)90048-2.

Guinart, M., & Grau, M. 2014. "Qualitative Analysis of the Short-Term and Long-Term Impact of Family Breakdown on Children: Case Study." *Journal Of Divorce & Remarriage*, *55*(5), 408–422. DOI: 10.1080/10502556.2014.920687.

Hines, A. M. 1997. "Divorce-related transitions, adolescent development, and the role of the parent-child relationship: A review of the literature." *Journal of Marriage and the Family*, 375–388.

Holmen, T. L. 1995. "Smoking and health in adolescence." *THE NORDTRØNDELAG HEALTH STUDY, 97.*

Huurre, T., Junkkari, H., & Aro, H. 2006. "Long-term psychosocial effects of parental divorce." *European archives of psychiatry and clinical neuroscience*, *256*(4), 256–263.

Jacobson, D. S. 1978. "The Impact of Marital Separation/Divorce on Children: I. Parent-Child Separation and Child Adjustment." *Journal of Divorce*, *1*(4), 341–360.

Jeynes, W. 2002. *Divorce, Family Structure, and the Academic Success of Children*. Binghamton, NY: Haworth Press, Inc.

Kaye, S. 1989. "The Impact of Divorce on Children's Academic Performance." *Journal Of Divorce*, *12*(2–3), 283–298. DOI: 10.1300/j279v12n02_16.

Kelly, J. B. 2000. "Children's adjustment in conflicted marriage and divorce: a decade review of research." *Journal of the American Academy of Child & Adolescent Psychiatry*, *39*(8), 963–973.

Kleinsorge, C., & Covitz, L. M. 2012. "Impact of divorce on children: developmental considerations." *Pediatrics in review*, *33*(4), 147–54.

Levitin, T. E. 1979. "Children of divorce: An introduction." *Journal of Social Issues.*

Rogers, F., & Judkis, J. 1996. *Let's Talk About It: Divorce*. Pittsburg, PA: Family Communications, Inc.

Rosen, R. 1979. "Some Crucial Issues Concerning Children of Divorce." *Journal Of Divorce*, *3*(1), 19–25. DOI: 10.1300/j279v03n01_02.

Rydelius, P. 1983. "Alcohol-abusing teenage boys." *Acta Psychiatrica Scandinavica*, *68*(5), 368–380. DOI: 10.1111/j.1600-0447.1983.tb07019.x.

Shinn, M. 1978. "Father absence and children's cognitive development." *Psychological Bulletin, 85*(2), 295–324.

Spruijt, E., & Duindam, V. 2005. "Problem Behavior of Boys and Young Men After Parental Divorce in the Netherlands." *Journal Of Divorce & Remarriage, 43*(3–4), 141–155. DOI: 10.1300/j087v43n03_08.

Størksen, I., Røysamb, E., Holmen, T. L., & Tambs, K. 2006. "Adolescent adjustment and well-being: Effects of parental divorce and distress." *Scandinavian journal of psychology, 47*(1), 75–84.

Tooley, K. 1976. "Antisocial behavior and social alienation: the "man of the house" and his mother."

"Violent behavior in teenage boys has been traced to two factors-complications in delivery and maternal rejection." 1995. *The Journal of the American Osteopathic Association, 95*(1), 19B. DOI: 10.7556/java.1995.95.1.19b.

Wallerstein, J. S. 1991. "The long-term effects of divorce on children: a review." *Journal of the American Academy of Child & Adolescent Psychiatry, 30*(3), 349–360.

Wauterickx, N., Gouwy, A., & Bracke, P. 2006. "Parental Divorce and Depression." *Journal Of Divorce & Remarriage, 45*(3–4), 43–68. DOI: 10.1300/j087v45n03_03.

Wyman, P. A., Cowen, E. L., Hightower, A. D., & Pedro-Carroll, J. L. 1985. "Perceived competence, self-esteem, and anxiety in latency-aged children of divorce." *Journal of Clinical Child Psychology, 14*, 20–26.

ABOUT THE AUTHOR

The author has graduated with associate of arts degree in psychology, BSc in psychology specializing in Christian psychology from Liberty University, BSc in psychology specializing in crisis Counseling, BSc in psychology specializing in life coaching, and master of arts (MA) in human services counselling specializing in addictions and recovery.

The author also has a diploma in biblical counseling, and he is a PhD candidate. He is pursuing his doctor of philosophy (PhD) in higher education administration specializing in education leadership. The author has completed his education and his diploma in biblical counseling from American Association of Christian Counselor (AACC), Live University. The credibility of his work is endorsed by the quality of institution that he was bred in. The love for humanity and the urge to develop an extensive narrative that intertwines concept of marriage, divorce, and religion are due to his extensive experience as a Christian counsellor. The author is a board-certified pastoral-care counselor, board-certified Christian counselor, board-certified Christian life coach, and board-certified biblical counselor. The author is a board member of Christian Life Coaching (BCLC), an advanced Christian life coach, and a master Christian life coach. The author is a board-certified biblical counselor.

The author also has broad range of certificates of completion authorized from Church Pastoral Center (CPC) Certification: Prepare/Enrich Certification in Acute Street, Grief and Trauma Breaking Free, Caring for Kids God's Way, Caring for People God's Way, Domestic and Community Crisis Response, Financial Coaching, Marriage Works Professional Life Coaching, Professional Life Coaching 201, and Stress and Trauma Care with Military Application. This broad range of certification overwhelms the author's ability to talk about a sensitive issue like marriage, especially with respect to the Christian perspective. The author has broad range of experiences in different fields, which is the reason the book serves an interdisciplinary purpose as the author uses psychological strings of men and women to connect them with religious narrative regarding marriage. The authority to discuss these concepts comes from the author's extensive experience and knowledge.